PlayTime® Piano

 Disney

LEVEL 1

Arranged by Nancy and Randall Faber

T0024258

This book belongs to: _____

Production Coordinator: Jon Ophoff
Editor: Isabel Otero Bowen
Design and Illustration: Terpstra Design, San Francisco
Engraving: Dovetree Productions, Inc.

FABER
PIANO ADVENTURES®

Hal•Leonard®

A NOTE TO TEACHERS

PlayTime® Piano Disney brings together contemporary and classic Disney hits arranged for the Level 1 pianist. In the words of Walt Disney, "There is more treasure in books than in all the pirates' loot on Treasure Island." This book offers musical treasure for piano students with blockbusters from *Coco, The Lion King, Frozen, Mary Poppins, Beauty and the Beast*, and more.

Students develop confidence at the piano through reading notes, intervals, and basic rhythms. *PlayTime® Piano* books explore these music concepts with inspiring songs.

PlayTime® Piano designates Level 1 of the PreTime to BigTime Piano Supplementary Library arranged by Faber and Faber. The series allows students to enjoy a favorite style at their current level of study. PlayTime books are available in these styles: *Popular, Classics, Jazz & Blues, Rock 'n Roll, Ragtime & Marches, Hymns, Kids' Songs, Christmas*, and the *Faber Studio Collection*.

Visit us at **PianoAdventures.com**.

Teacher Duets

Optional teacher duets are a valuable feature of the *PlayTime Piano* series. Although the arrangements stand complete on their own, the duets provide a fullness of harmony and rhythmic vitality. And not incidentally, they offer the opportunity for parent and student to play together.

Helpful Hints:

1. The student should know his or her part thoroughly before the teacher duet is used. Accurate rhythm is especially important.

2. Rehearsal numbers are provided to give the student and teacher starting places.

3. The teacher may wish to count softly a measure aloud before beginning, as this will help the ensemble.

THE PRETIME TO BIGTIME PIANO LIBRARY

PreTime® Piano   =   Primer Level

PlayTime® Piano   =   Level 1

ShowTime® Piano   =   Level 2A

ChordTime® Piano   =   Level 2B

FunTime® Piano   =   Level 3A–3B

BigTime® Piano   =   Level 4 & above

ISBN 978-1-61677-698-5

Printed in U.S.A.

TABLE OF CONTENTS

4

Hand Position

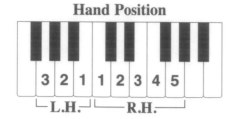

L.H.   R.H.

Part of Your World
from *The Little Mermaid*

WHO SAID THIS?
Flounder, don't be
such a guppy.

Music by ALAN MENKEN
Lyrics by HOWARD ASHMAN

Moderately fast

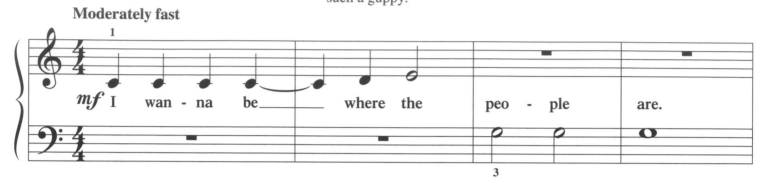

mf I wan - na be_____ where the peo - ple are.

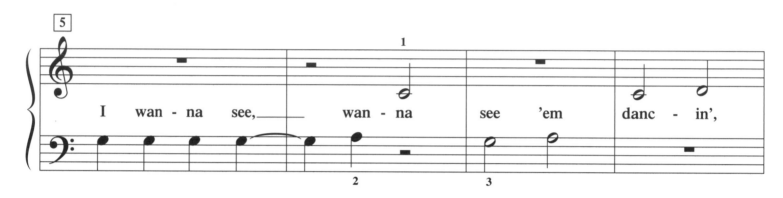

I wan - na see,_____ wan - na see 'em danc - in',

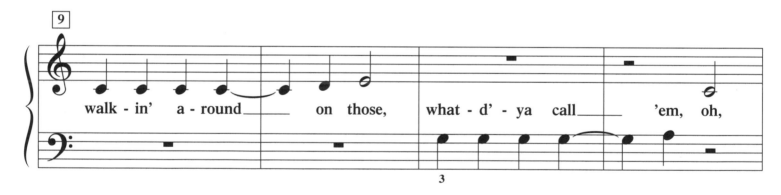

walk - in' a - round_____ on those, what - d' - ya call_____ 'em, oh,

Teacher Duet: (Student plays 1 octave higher)

R.H.

L.H.

mp

FF3040

FF3040

6

Hand Position

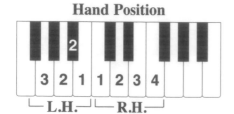

A Spoonful of Sugar
from *Mary Poppins*

WHO SAID THIS?
We'd better keep
an eye on this one.
She's tricky.

Words and Music by
RICHARD M. SHERMAN
and ROBERT B. SHERMAN

Cheerfully

L.H.

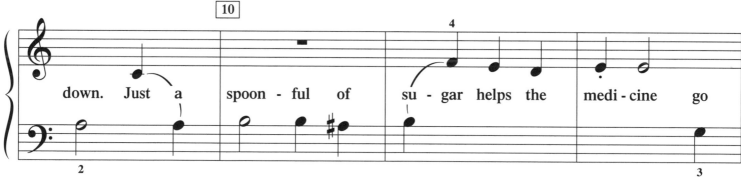

Teacher Duet: (Student plays 1 octave higher)

FF3040

Hand Position

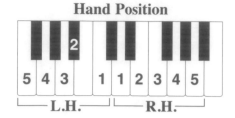

Let's Go Fly a Kite
from *MARY POPPINS*

WHO SAID THIS?
Spit-spot!

Words and Music by
RICHARD M. SHERMAN
and ROBERT B. SHERMAN

Moderately fast

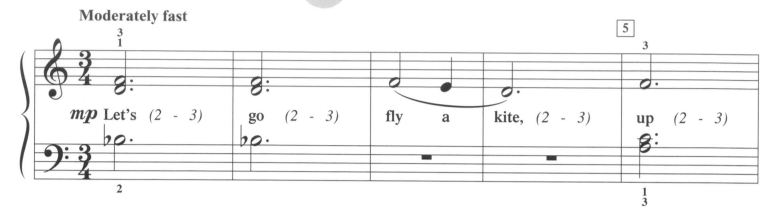

mp Let's *(2 - 3)* go *(2 - 3)* fly a kite, *(2 - 3)* up *(2 - 3)*

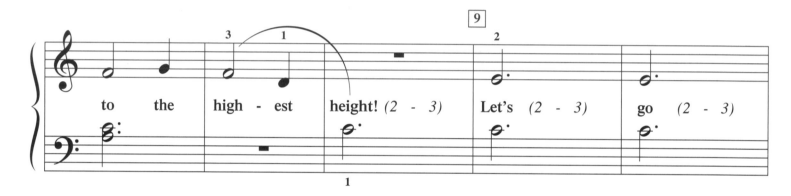

to the high - est height! *(2 - 3)* Let's *(2 - 3)* go *(2 - 3)*

Teacher Duet: (Student plays 1 octave higher)

Beauty and the Beast

from *Beauty and the Beast*

Music by ALAN MENKEN
Lyrics by HOWARD ASHMAN

WHO SAID THIS?
True, that he's no Prince Charming, but there's something in him that I simply didn't see.

Teacher Duet: (Student plays 1 octave higher)

11

ANSWER: Belle

FF3040

12

Hand Position

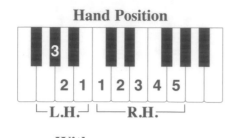

WHO SAID THIS?
How can you read this?
There's no pictures!

Gaston
from BEAUTY AND THE BEAST

Music by ALAN MENKEN
Lyrics by HOWARD ASHMAN

With energy

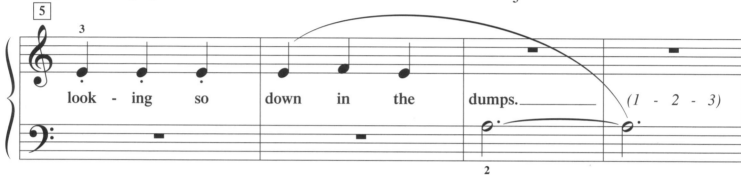

Teacher Duet: (Student plays 1 octave higher)

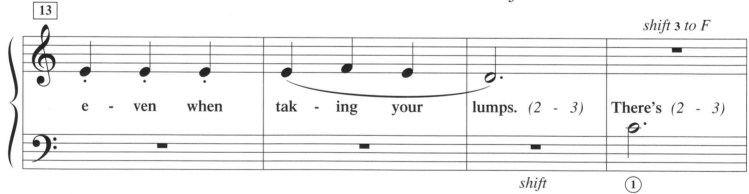

(Contains previously unreleased lyrics from Howard Ashman)

Remember Me
(Ernesto de la Cruz)
from *Coco*

WHO SAID THIS?
I didn't wanna listen, but he was right…nothing is more important than family.

Words and Music by
KRISTEN ANDERSON-LOPEZ
and **ROBERT LOPEZ**

16

Moderately

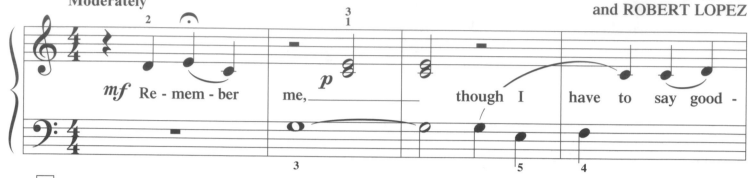

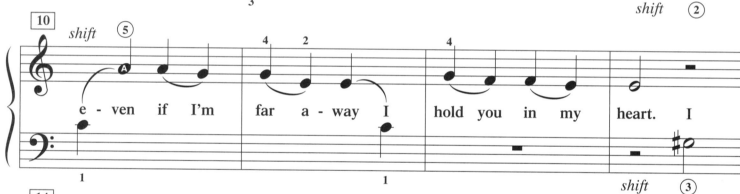

Teacher Duet: (Student plays 1 octave higher)

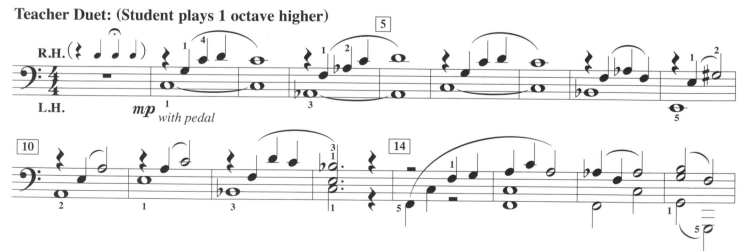

Hand Position

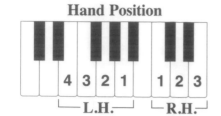

I Just Can't Wait to Be King
from *The Lion King*

Music by ELTON JOHN
Lyrics by TIM RICE

Moderately fast

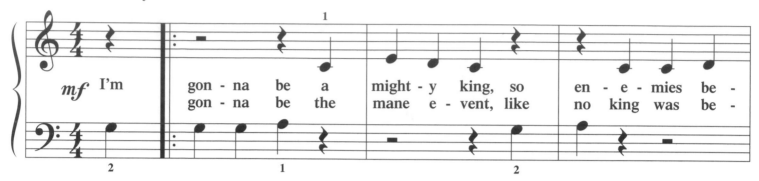

mf I'm gon - na be a might - y king, so en - e - mies be -
gon - na be the mane e - vent, like no king was be -

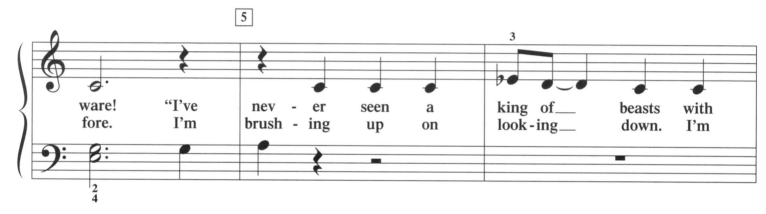

ware! "I've nev - er seen a king of__ beasts with
fore. I'm brush - ing up on look - ing__ down. I'm

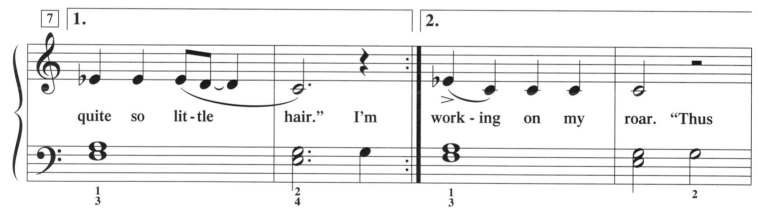

1. quite so lit - tle hair." I'm
2. work - ing on my roar. "Thus

Teacher Duet: (Student plays 1 octave higher)

19

WHO SAID THIS?
Oh yes, the past can hurt. But the way I see it,
you can either run from it, or learn from it.

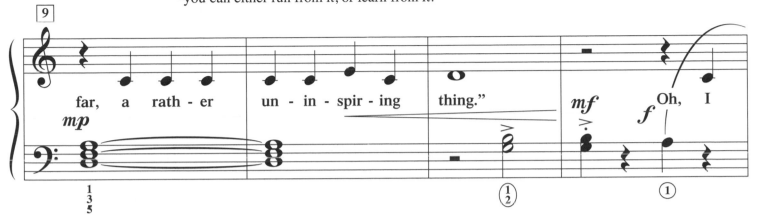

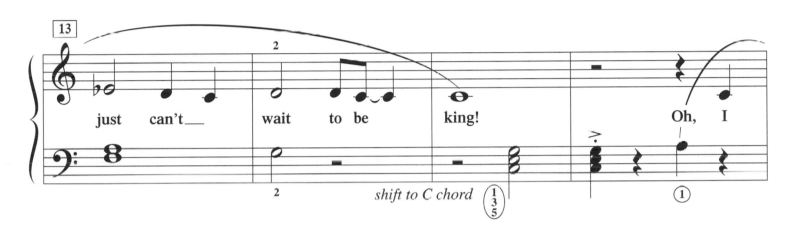

far, a rath - er un - in - spir - ing thing." *mf* *f* Oh, I
mp

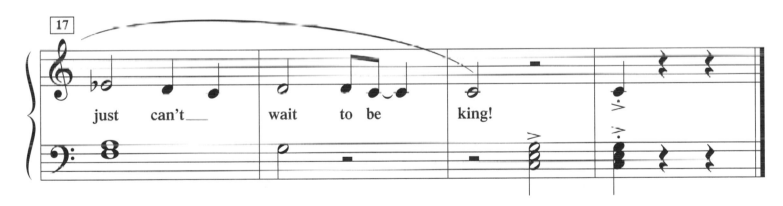

just can't___ wait to be king! Oh, I
shift to C chord

just can't___ wait to be king!

ANSWER: Rafiki

FF3040

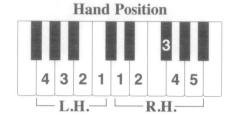

Hand Position

Gummi Bears Theme

from *Adventures of the Gummi Bears*

WHO SAID THIS?
Cubbi, the way to solve problems
is to charge right in!

Words and Music by
MICHAEL SILVERSHER
and **PATTY SILVERSHER**

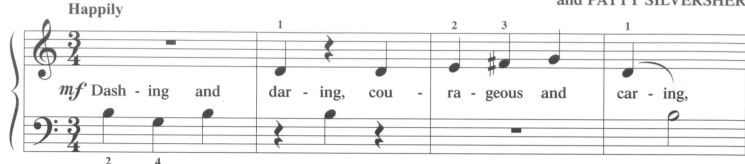

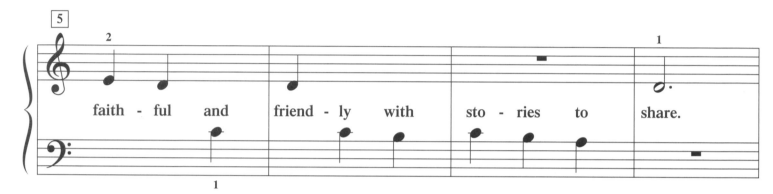

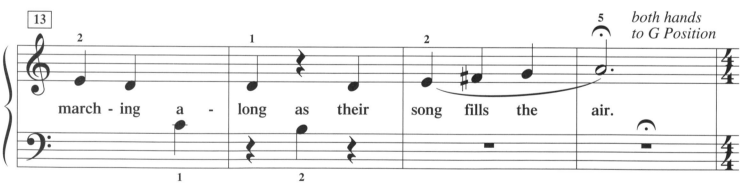

Teacher Duet: (Student plays 1 octave higher)

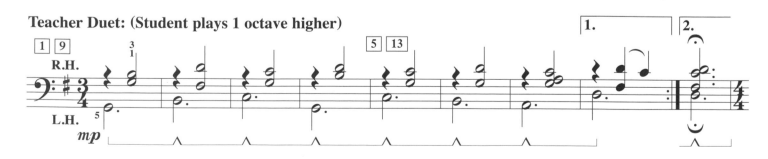

Let It Go

from *FROZEN*

WHO SAID THIS?
You kind of set off an
eternal winter…everywhere.

Music and Lyrics by
KRISTEN ANDERSON-LOPEZ
and ROBERT LOPEZ

Moderately slow

The snow glows white on the moun-tain to - night, not a

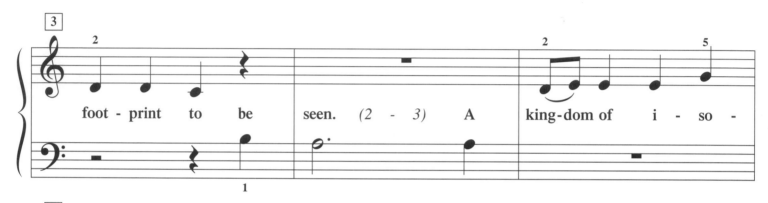

foot - print to be seen. *(2 - 3)* A king-dom of i - so -

la - tion, and it looks like I'm the queen. *(1 - 2 - 3 - 4)*

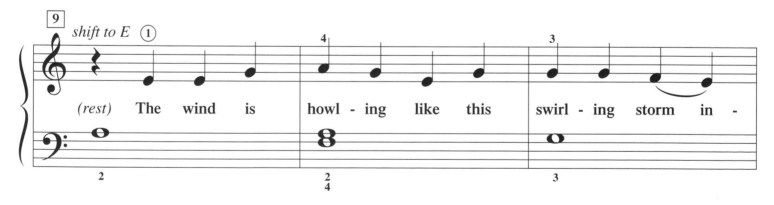

shift to E ①

(rest) The wind is howl - ing like this swirl - ing storm in -

Teacher Duet: (Student plays 1 octave higher)

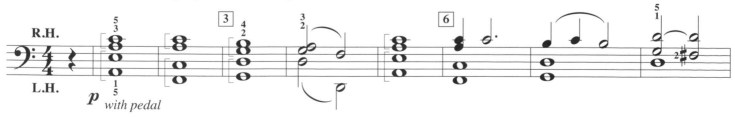

R.H.

L.H. *p with pedal*

23

ANSWER: Anna

FF3040